My stream of consciousness: a collection of poems from an early age

Allie Steemson

India | USA | UK

Presentation by *BookLeaf Publishing*

Web: www.bookleafpub.com

E-mail: info@bookleafpub.com

ISBN: 9789358736069

First edition 2023

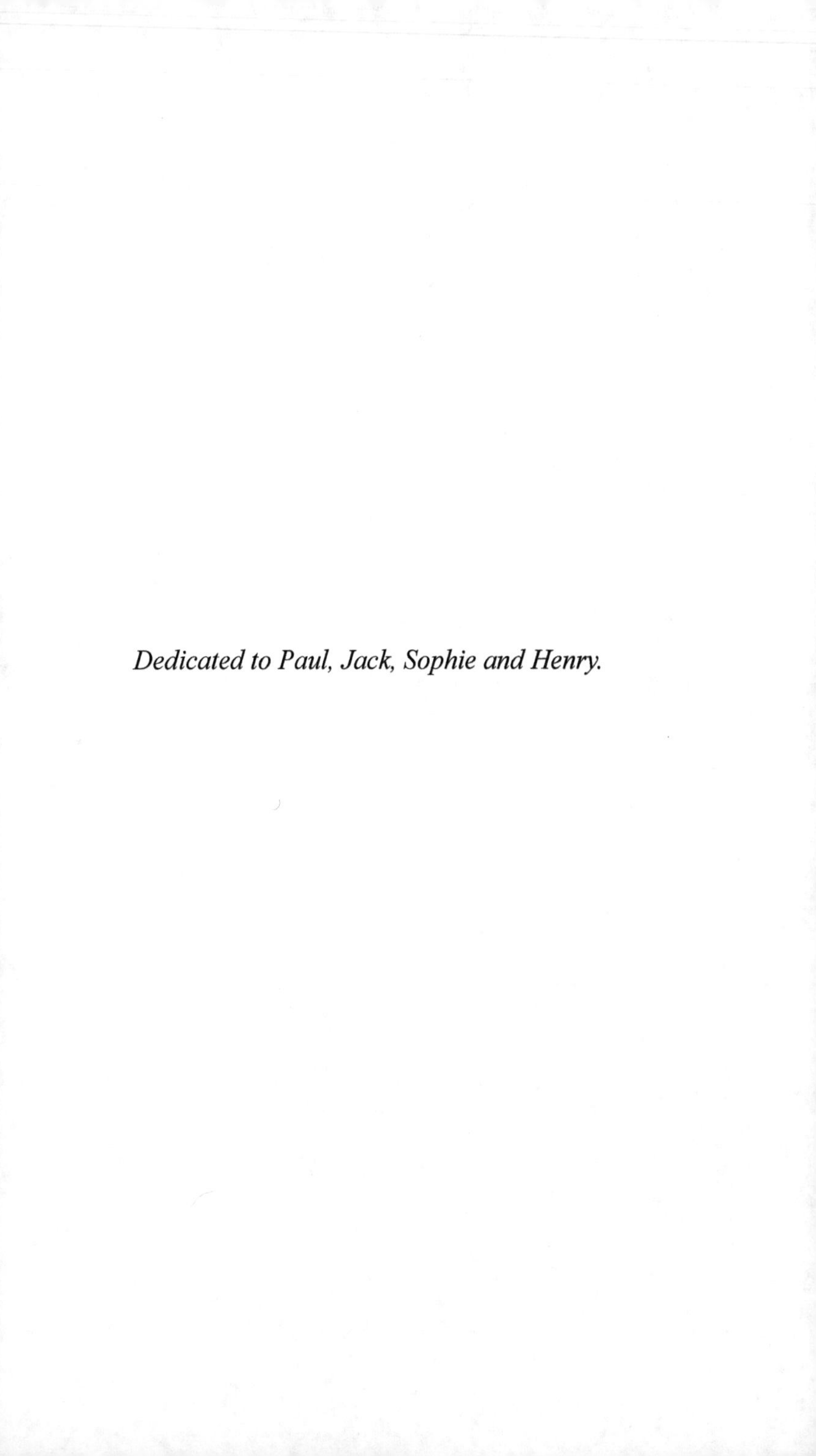

Dedicated to Paul, Jack, Sophie and Henry.

ACKNOWLEDGEMENT

I want to thank my wonderful husband Paul, for his patience and hard-work, which helps our family to function on a daily basis; I love him eternally . I also want to thank my lovely friends Adele and Emma, with whom I can always talk about real feelings. I also want to thank my inspirational friend (and author) Ruth Kelly, who makes me laugh so much!

The Flower Show

Flowers, crafts are all now here,
The Flower Show comes every year.
Cakes and cookies,
Biscuits and cheese,
Geraniums, roses and sweet peas.

I really enjoy the Flower Show,
And every year,
I love to go!

(aged 8)

Medusa

Never go to the edge of the world,
As you'll find Medusa there.
With flame red eyes,
And a look that can kill,
And poisonous snakes for her hair.

(aged 10)

Sunset

As the sun goes down,
On the ploughed fields brown,
And the evening slips away,
We turn our eyes,
To the amber skies,
And dream of another day.

(aged 15)

A bad chicken called Bob

A chicken, quite boldly, walked into a pub,
Looked at the land-lord,
And demanded some grub.

The Land-lord stopped serving,
And starred in surprise,
At the irate chicken before his eyes.

"GIVE ME SOME GRUB!",
It said with a glare,
"I WANT STEAK, CHIPS and PEAS,
COOKED MEDIUM RARE!"

Now the land-lord didn't flinch,
Didn't scream, didn't shout.
He just picked up that chicken,
And drop-kicked it out!

(aged 15)

My pencil case

My pencil case,
Was in a race,
He won first place,
Had a smile on his face!

(aged 15)

If I were a pigeon

If I were a pigeon,
I would fly,
High up into the sky.

I'd sit on famous statues,
And poo on passers-by.

(aged 15)

The joys of Geography revision

I hate revising,
It is s**t,
I'd rather sleep, or lie, or sit
Upon this bed,
But all that said,
I'd best return to brown and red…
…soil

(aged 17)

My dear friend, please forgive this poem!

My dear friend Valentine,
Is happy all the time,
And I'm the only one who knows,
That this is down to wine!

She drinks it in the classroom,
She drinks it in the house,
But nobody suspects her,
(she's as quiet as a mouse).

And have you ever noticed that her nose is
always red,
And she really cannot walk straight,
Down a wrong path you've been led.

She's such a lovely, pleasant girl,
Is what you used to think ,
But now you know her better,
She's a servant of the drink!

(aged 17)

Henry

Henry is squishy and cuddly and mad,
He's the person to cheer you if ever you're sad.
He loves a good dance at all times of the day,
And follows his sister wherever they play.

He's determined and dextrous,
And cheeky and happy,
And ridiculously wiggly, when changing his
nappy.

We love him and will guide him, as best as we
can,
Our gorgeous and happy,
Tiny ginger man.

(2018)

A poem about starting counselling training

Metal chairs,
Bitten hairs,
Through the hall and by the stairs.
Please be kind,
Please like me!
This is who I want to be.

All my life,
Through the strife,
All those boulders in my way.
Now I'm here,
I feel fear,
Can I do this anyway?

(2021)

Hope

A glimpse of hope,
Of something else,
Of something I have dreamed or wished or
wanted,
Forever it seems.

Something I have always felt,
Have always known.

Talking helps people,
Kindness helps people,
Trust yourself.

Trust yourself to learn,
Trust yourself to practice,
Rome wasn't built in a day.
You'll get there because you want to.

(2021)

Change

Learning,
Yearning,
Searching,
Finding….
Myself,
Through this process of change.

But change for me is often scary.
Could it be less so?

A growing, more knowing, skills showing
Tentatively glowing….?

(2021)

My Kids are doing the washing: on starting my Doctorate.

My kids are doing the washing,
It isn't hard to see,
That they are clearly doing,
Much much better than me.

I'm crying much more lately,
And kicking cupboard doors,
And punching my nice cushions,
And sleeping on the floor.

My kids are doing the washing,
And putting themselves to bed,
Their getting all their school work done,
Can they do mine instead?

I feel like I've been captured,
By an evil conjurer,
That makes me do things I don't like,
And asks for more and more.

My kids are doing the washing,
But I'm very proud of them,

They keep me sane and happy,
Despite the 1 a m.

(2022)

A Poem about my beautiful mother-in-law, Marie

You are gone and I miss you,
Wish you were here again,
Cannot believe that I'll never see you,
Never see your smiling face.

Sophie's sad and wants hugs,
So do I if I am honest,
Picture Henry in your arms,
Holding you tight.

All the images I have,
Want them to stay forever,
Wish I could hold onto them,
Wish I could speak with you,
And tell you all our news.

You are gone,
And I miss you,
Miss the gentle conversation,
Miss your sunshine and your care.
Miss the love you had for Paul,
Miss the love you had for all.

(2022)

Discovering dyspraxia

Oh my life!
I can't believe,
It's finally getting done,
I've spent my life just wandering,
What life was like for some.

How do you find your way around?
How do you get there quick?
I'm always late, I'm always lost,
I'm always feeling 'thick'.

The tears are coming,
They're sitting there,
Right now behind my eyes.

I want to feel so liberated,
But all I feel is sad,
Sad for all the times I felt so dumb, frustrated,
mad.

Other people don't get so lost,
Don't find it had to process…
All that data, all those numbers.

But I did,

I do.

Thankful for others to help me,
To help me understand,

I need to cry,
To see that little girl,
And hold her hand.

You couldn't add up the numbers,
That would not stay inside your head.
You couldn't find your classes,
You had to ask instead.

But it's ok,
You're not alone,
You've got Pat and Kate and Tom.
They will be there to help you through
To know that you're not just 'wrong'

(2023)

Do I continue my Doctorate?

I am so fucking tired,
And I really need to sleep,
But I need to stop,
For a whole entire week.

But I feel that I cannot,
There's so much work to do!
In my house,
In my reading,
Oh and the shopping too!

I've forgotten the food order,
I've got to clean the pigs,
My son is hyperactive,
I just want to hold my kids.

Is this course really worth it?
Could I be just as pleased,
With being a therapist,
Who uses art…..

Who fucking knows,
It's gone midnight,
And I really need to sleep.

(2023, and yes, I've postponed my Doctorate!)

To my little Girl, on her 8th Birthday

Born on a pillow,
In the middle of the floor,
My darling little girl,
I just couldn't love you more.

You're kind and you're playful,
And you're crazy,
And you're sweet.
You really are, my little girl,
The best you'd ever meet.

I am privileged to know you,
You have made my life more real.
Before I had you, I never knew,
How much my heart could feel.

So thank you little Sophie,
For the fun, the love, the play,
And enjoy this celebration,
Of your extra special day.

Love from Mummy x x x

(2023)

Honey Bear

We passed him every day for school,
A jar for storing honey.
"Can we buy him?",
(Every day!),
"Can we buy him Mummy?".

I'm not quite sure,
I have not checked,
I have not any money.
I'm sorry kids,
We cannot buy the bear-shaped jar of honey.

But then that day we passed again,
And a thought flashed in my mind,
I'd found a five-pound note that morn,
I'd found one on the side.

Triumphantly I said to them,
"Guess what, I have some money!",
And we rushed to grab that very special,
Bear-shaped jar of honey.

Now 'Honey-Bear' stands proudly,
At the back of our old range,

And the children asked if I could write a poem
in his name.

So here it is,
This one's for you.
You really are so yummy.
A very special, bear-shaped jar of tasty, golden
honey.

(2023)

My Favourite Field

When I'm sad I like to wander,
And to shout out,
And then to ponder,
With my dog just calmly patient,
In my very favourite field.

Then I've vented,
And I'm walking,
Sometimes thinking,
Sometimes talking,
To my dog,
Or just my own self,
In my very favourite field.

I see beetles in the grass,
And the swallows sometimes pass,
Above my head,
Above my troubles,
In my very favourite field.

There's the river,
Always flowing,
Always a comfort,
Always knowing,
Distracting me from worries,

In my very favourite field.

It's my own place,
It's a friend,
It makes me smile,
(By the end),
It's my daily soothing dog-walk,
In my very favourite field.

(2023)

Flu

I have the flu,
It's really poo,
I've been retching in my bathroom loo,
And haven't slept since half past two.

It's made my dreams,
Really horrid,
And made my flushed cheeks very florid,
I hope to maybe sleep tonight,
But it's starting to get light.

I'm better today,
Hurrah, Hooray!

I can sit at my PC,
I even ate some toast for tea!
I hope it's gone now for a bit,
'Cos having flu is really… rather inconvenient.

(2023)

Poppy

We have a spaniel,
Who eats our shoes,
Who likes to laze,
Who likes to snooze.

She is so pretty,
She's our best mate,
She goes insane,
By our back gate.

She loves the pheasant,
She loves the fox,
I wish she didn't ,
Love our socks.

(2023)